Why Did Jesus Have to Die?

A Biblical Study of Salvation
and the
Theological Implications of

Jesus

As
*The Truly Perfect
Substitutionary Blood Sacrifice*

Why Did Jesus Have to Die?

A Biblical Study of Salvation
and the
Theological Implications of

Jesus

As
*The Truly Perfect
Substitutionary Blood Sacrifice*

T. B. Thornton, Th. M.

Copyright © 2025 by T. B. Thornton, Th.M. All rights reserved.

All scripture references are taken from the New King James Version®. Copyright © 1982 by Thomas Nelson. Used by permission. All rights reserved

Printed in the United States of America

Publishing services by Selah Publishing Group, LLC, Tennessee. The views expressed or implied in this work do not necessarily reflect those of Selah Publishing Group.

No part of this publication may be reproduced, stored in a retrieval system or transmitted in any way by any means, electronic, mechanical, photocopy, recording or otherwise, without the prior permission of the author except as provided by USA copyright law, and except by a reviewer who may quote brief passages in a review to be printed in a newspaper, magazine or journal.

ISBN: 978-1-58930-327-0
Library of Congress Control Number: 2025906849

Contents

Foreword 7

Chapter One
Faith in the Old and New Testaments........................ 11

Chapter Two
Why Did Jesus Have to Die? Part 1............................. 17

Chapter Three
A Substitute is Provided 25

Chapter Four
Why Did Jesus Have to Die? Part 2 31

Chapter Five
What Did Jesus' Sacrifice Accomplish? 35

Chapter Six
The Process of Salvation; Part 1 41

Chapter Seven
The Process of Salvation; Part 2 51

Chapter Eight
The Security of the Believer's Salvation 57

Chapter Nine
What Salvation is Not 63

Chapter Ten
The Hope We Have in Christ! 71

For a Deeper Study 79

Order Information 81

Foreword

As Christians, and as we grow in our understanding of Scripture, a problem automatically arises: to fully comprehend the entire scope of our faith in all areas involved, we must find a way of compartmentalizing the many facets of the unknowable God we strive to know. Otherwise, we are overwhelmed by the sheer enormity of an endless enigma. In times of worship and personal reflection, a childlike faith helps us to be in the proper state of mind where the intricacies of our faith are less important than merely being still and knowing that God is who He says He is. This pleases God, and He rewards us by watering our souls with a sense of peace, tranquility, and inspiration that is sorely needed in our busy, cluttered lives.

However, it also pleases God when we delve into His Word and study. For this is how He reveals Himself to us; He gives us a little at a time, opening our eyes only to what we can handle (or need to know) at that moment so as not to overwhelm and confuse us. As we gain understanding and strive to share our faith with others, it becomes more necessary for us to learn the deeper things of our faith—to strive to know our unknowable God. We do this, not to lord our knowledge over others, but to settle the harder aspects of faith within ourselves and to know how to answer questions from those with which we are sharing our faith.

I have spent many years of deep theological study in the hopes of understanding everything about the Creator. It is rather humorous to me now, that I ever thought such a thing was possible. What I found was this: the more I know, the more I know I don't know! However, at the same time, I *have* managed to grasp many truths that, quite frankly, leave me stunned at the lengths the Creator has gone to show us His boundless, eternal love.

Not the least of these truths are the Doctrines of Salvation (in theological terms, *Soteriology*). In fact, of all the disciplines of Systematic Theology (of which there are ten, all with long and boring names I won't make you suffer through here), the doctrines surrounding salvation are integral to all the others. If one studies the Doctrines of the Church, salvation is the initiation rite. If one studies the Doctrines of Sin, salvation is the cure. If one studies the Doctrines of Man, salvation is the greatest gift God has given him!

Therefore, we will endeavor to make a precise study of the Doctrine of Salvation for two reasons: First, the Great Commission calls all of us to do our part in spreading the Good News of Christ to all who will listen. Those efforts take shape in different ways for different people. As my callings are teaching and writing, this is one way I can contribute to the spread of the Gospel.

The second reason for this study is more specific. I have been teaching in one capacity or another within my church for several years. In so doing, I have come to recognize a significant lack of fundamental, doctrinal understanding among the people within the church. In polling others who belong to different congregations, I have found that the same deficit of biblical understanding (and, in many cases, literacy) exists within the rest of the visible church (both local and national). The wrong ideas of the world have infiltrated the minds of believers to a degree that, frankly, astounded me. For example, when I asked questions about the role of angels, some answers had more in common with a theology based upon Frank Capra's classic, *It's a Wonderful Life*, than those based in Scripture.

However, perhaps the saddest response came when I asked my students why Jesus had to die for our sins. The answers were, at best, muddled and confused. Frighteningly, some of the answers were even anti-Semitic (a troubling trend within today's church). The unfortunate reality is that, while I did not expect the students to hold doctorates in theology, it became clear that pop culture seems to inform the church of today to a greater degree than Scripture. More than that, popular notions in media hold more sway over the believers than solid Biblical teaching. In my church, I listen to the same sermons they do—theologically sound sermons. Yet, those same believers still hold to the unsound teachings of the world. Perhaps this is because they spend more time listening to the sermons of the world than sermons delivered in church.

The root of most of these issues, however, is something that each Christian must strive to correct: A severe lack of daily Bible reading at home. The God and Creator of the universe has gone to great lengths to communicate His love to us. The very least we can do is read His love letter. If you are reading this, it means that you are making an effort to learn. And, if you meditate on the biblical truths within these pages, the benefits of what you find will change the way you see and live out your faith.

At any rate, the purpose of this study is to present a clear and informative teaching on the subject of salvation geared toward the church laity, presented much as a Bible college student at an Associate's level would expect to receive. If I achieve my goals, the reader/student should be able to do three things based on the information contained herein:

1. The reader/student should be able to come to a biblically solid understanding of their salvation within themselves, thus giving them a new and greater desire to praise God for this greatest of gifts.

2. The student should be able to clearly explain these concepts to other believers when confronted with the erroneous, confused theology of the world that has infiltrated the modern church.

3. Based upon their new understanding, the student should be able to clearly and intelligently share the Gospel of Jesus Christ, thus fulfilling the Great Commission.

An Important Note from the Author

As I discuss what God requires for our salvation, I want to make perfectly clear one very critical fact: I in no way ascribe to the ever-increasing, popular notion of "super-grace." This is the idea that because God's grace is so great, we can live as carnal and godless a lifestyle as we wish and remain in God's good graces. That is the furthest thing from the truth! In fact, if you believe you have accepted Jesus as your Savior, yet you have a desire to go on sinning as if nothing had happened, then I would suggest that nothing has happened to change you from unsaved to saved. A person who has become a new creature in Christ, though they may still struggle with sin, no longer *wants* to go on sinning. However, if you are one of those who do, you may do well to study Jesus' "parable of the wedding feast" in Matt. 22:1-14, paying special attention to the guest who was not properly attired (having not put on Jesus' righteousness).

Chapter One

Faith in the Old and New Testaments

Old Testament

Many believers today tend to think of salvation as a post-empty-tomb concept based on the fact that Jesus' death, burial, and resurrection had not yet happened in Old Testament times. However, the impetus for salvation is not so much the *fact* of Jesus' death, burial, and resurrection as it is *faith* in Jesus and the atonement accomplished through His death, burial, and resurrection. The question then becomes, "If faith in Jesus is the requirement for salvation, and Jesus had not yet come, how could the Old Testament saints have attained salvation?"

The answer is the same for them as it is for us today: "Faith in the Messiah."

We are so blessed that we can read the Gospels about Jesus' life and see what He did for us on that Cross. (I capitalize Cross because I view it as a proper noun—an important physical and historically significant place in time and space.) Though faith for many comes with some difficulty, if at all, we are still blessed to have the ability to look at the completed Passion of Christ and read the eyewitness accounts of what was accomplished there.

Just imagine how much more difficult it would be to have faith in a Messiah that had not yet come. Yet, that is precisely what the Old Testament saints had to do—devote themselves to God and place their faith in the promised Messiah.

The Fall of Man, which occurred in the Garden of Eden, was the point at which God first announced His plan. Of course, though God knew from eternity past what His plan would involve, until sin entered the world through Adam there was no need to reveal it. However, with the dreadful deed done, God immediately extended hope to the Garden's now cursed and distraught inhabitants when He laid down His indictment on the serpent:

> *"And I will put enmity between you and the woman, and between your seed and her Seed; He shall bruise your head, and you shall bruise His heel."* Gen. 3:15

Many scholars refer to this verse as the *protoevangelium* (*proto* meaning "first" and *evangelium* meaning "gospel"). In other words, God was prophesying the coming of One who would be born of the seed of a woman and offer an answer for the curse of sin. So it is that in the following millennia, from Adam to Enoch and Noah, from Abraham to Moses and David, and down through Malachi (the heroes of the faith, so eloquently listed and described by the writer of Hebrews in chapter 11), put their saving faith in God's promise of a Messiah—a Messiah they would never know in a temporal sense. Yet, they knew Him in an intimately spiritual sense due to their great faith in the God who promised His coming.

It is in that fantastic spiritual reality that we, in this day, can find great hope and comfort. By that, I mean to say that though we, flawed and sinful as we are (not unlike the imperfect and sinful saints of the Old Testament), get so many things wrong and fall so many times, our salvation was not earned through our merits, but through faith in the One who sacrificed Himself for such sinful men.

> *"These all died in faith, not having received the promises, but having seen them afar off were assured of them, embraced them and confessed that they were strangers and pilgrims on the earth."* Heb. 11:13

A Word About the Law

The Mosaic Law (the Ten Commandments, later broken into the 613 Levitical Laws) was never so much meant to be a guide to the way of salvation. However, the vast majority of the "religious leaders" of the Old Testament acted as though it was. While it was true that if one could manage to live out a perfect earthly existence (following not only the letter of the Law but the spirit of the Law as well), their salvation could be achieved, no mortal human could ever accomplish that. Since the sin nature passes through the seed of Adam, and all of humanity is born of Adam's seed, all are born into sin (this will be further delineated later). Therefore, for any mortal man to follow the Law perfectly was an impossible pursuit.

Why, then, would God have given Israel the Law if it were impossible for man to follow it effectively? The answer is twofold:

1. First, God gave Israel the Law so they would be set apart from the heathen nations around them and so, in their efforts to follow it, they would live a better existence and be bound by natural, ethical, and social standards, reflecting God's goodness in how His people treated each other and governed their lives.

2. Second, the very impossibility of effectively following the Law served to point out the fact that humanity was in desperate need of a Savior. Along with the Law, Israel also had the promises of a coming Messiah who *could* fulfill the humanly impossible requirements of the Law. Israel was never meant to put their faith in the Law. Rather, they were to put their faith in the One who would fulfill the Law on man's behalf.

Note 1: I intentionally did not address the sacrificial system within the Law in this section. That system was part of the Law as a whole. Therefore, when I say "the Law," the sacrificial system is naturally included. In *Chapter 2, "Why Did Jesus Have to Die?"* the sacrificial system becomes a more relevant issue and will be discussed more explicitly.

Note 2: Without getting too far affield, I need to point out the fact that Old Testament (pre-empty-tomb) saints, upon death, did not go directly to Heaven as we New Covenant saints do. Their destination was a paradise-like holding place called "the Bosom of Abraham," (Luke 16:22-26) where they awaited the promised Messiah, who would lead "captivity captive," (Eph. 4:8) so they could go to Heaven to be with Him. This place was necessary because, as Jesus said, "No man can come to the Father except through Me." (John 14:6b) Therefore, though their salvation was secure, they had to await His finished work before they could proceed to Heaven. Jesus, during the three days His body was in the tomb, was leading those Old Testament saints out of the Bosom of Abraham and took them with Him to Heaven when He rose again. They apparently made a short stop with Jesus in Jerusalem before proceeding to Heaven. Jesus showed Himself to Mary Magdalene, telling her not to touch Him because He hadn't yet ascended to the Father. (John 20: 11-18) This explains what is described in Matt. 27:50-53 when several Old Testament saints were seen in Jerusalem.

To be clear, this view is not held by all theologians. However, in my opinion, it is the only view that satisfies all Scriptural references without contradiction.

New Testament

Having established above that the salvation of the Old Testament saints was based on faith in the promised Messiah, it becomes necessary to point out the fact that, though He had come as promised in the Gospel accounts, until He had suffered the Cross, His work was not yet finished. Therefore, the exact same salvation requirements were in effect during the 33 years of Christ's life on earth. And, to put a finer point on things, salvation as we know it (in which, when we place our faith in Christ, we are immediately adopted as sons and daughters, indwelt by the Holy Spirit, and become a part of the Church—the "Body of Christ") was not possible until the birth of the Church documented in Acts, chapter 2. In fact, one could argue that the more critical moment came when Jesus rose from the grave, conquering death and Hell forever. But those are arguments for another day.

Nevertheless, the faith requirement for salvation did not change after the Church's birth. Boiled down, the only difference between the saving faith of the Old Testament saints and the New Testament saints lies in the perspective of the saint. That is to say, while the Old Testament saint looked forward to a coming Messiah, the saints that came after the Event (the death, burial, and resurrection of Jesus) had the ability to look back and put their faith in what Jesus had already done. Therefore, both Old and New Testament saints were placing faith in the Messiah's accomplishments at the same Event.

Why Did Jesus Have to Die?

Discussion Questions

1. Do you believe that faith in the Old Testament days would have been harder to hold onto than today?

2. If so, does that give you a better appreciation for the faith of Enoch, Noah, Abraham, or David?

3. When was it that you realized that it was simple faith, not the Law, works, or your ability to be good enough that provided your salvation?

4. Knowing this, how freeing is it that your salvation doesn't depend on your ability to do good works in order to keep it?

Chapter Two

Why Did Jesus Have to Die? Part 1

As I mentioned in the introduction, this question became the impetus for my choice of subjects to write about in this study. I believe that if a person can answer this question intelligently, and of course, Scripturally, they will find that the whole of the Gospel becomes crystal clear. In fact, so important was this Event that even our perception of historical dating marks it (B. C./A. D.). Therefore, the reason—the necessity—for this Event surely warrants special attention. However, to fully understand the Event and why it had to happen, we need to go back to the Garden of Eden.

The Difference Between Physical Death and Spiritual Death

When God placed Adam and Eve in the Garden, they were perfectly alive, both physically and spiritually. By this, I mean to say that they were capable of living forever in a physical sense. They were also meant to enjoy perfect spiritual communion with God forever, knowing Him intimately in a way that we cannot fully grasp until we experience the Beatific Vision (The vision they enjoyed in the Garden, as well as the one we shall receive upon arrival in Heaven when our minds are unclouded by sin, and which allows us to perfectly see God for who He is). Their minds were not yet tainted by anything that would skew their view of who God is.

> *"Then the LORD God took the man and put him in the Garden of Eden to tend and keep it. And the LORD God commanded the man, saying, 'Of every tree of the garden you may freely eat; but of the tree of the knowledge of good and evil you shall not eat, for in the day that you eat of it you shall surely die.'"* Gen. 2:15-17

In the verses above, God had given Adam the one and only law which he was to follow. He also informed Adam of the penalty for disobeying that law: death. Now, when we read a bit further in the story, we eventually find the serpent (actually, Satan in the appearance of a serpent) tempting Eve:

> *"Then the serpent said to the woman, 'You will not surely die. For God knows that in the day you eat of it your eyes will be opened, and you will be like God, knowing good and evil.'"* Gen. 3:4-5

Like many of Satan's lies, this was a half-truth, which is, in reality, a whole lie. It is important to notice that God did not say, "*on* that day you shall surely die." He said, "*in* that day…" (v. 17). "On that day" would mean they would die the instant they ate of the fruit, but "in that day" meant an unspecified period of time, like saying, "back in the day." The serpent's implication was a slick intimation that "*on* that day" was what God meant. So, the question is, did they "surely die" when they ate the fruit? The answer is two-fold.

In the physical sense, though death did not occur immediately, the *process* of physical death and decay began immediately. Therefore, "in that day..." becomes a perfectly accurate statement. In the spiritual sense, the perfect communion with God they had enjoyed before instantly ended. They had passed from spiritual life to spiritual death. Therefore, in this way, "*on* that day" being included as part of "*in* that day" would be perfectly accurate. Nevertheless, no matter how you want to say it, man became spiritually dead. Man had lost his ability to commune with a perfect God and was now eternally separated from God. However, as alluded to in the previous section, God promised them that He would provide a Solution in the form of a Man who would bridge the gap (The *protoevangelium* from Gen. 3:15).

The Importance of Blood

The first animal sacrifice recorded in Scripture also occurs in Genesis. Just before driving Adam and Eve from Eden, God performed the sacrifice Himself:

> "*Also for Adam and his wife the LORD God made tunics of skin, and clothed them.*" Gen. 3:21

Though not implicitly stated, the skin had to have come from an animal, and the animal had to lose its life for that to be accomplished. Thus, blood was spilled in order to cover man's shame (sin). This was God's way of forgiving their transgression against Him. However, that did not mean the penalty for that transgression was no longer in effect. There is a difference between forgiveness and complete exoneration (as if it had never happened). This vital concept will become central to later discussions in this study. Therefore, a further illustration may help us to fully understand:

Why Did Jesus Have to Die?

Forgiveness vs. Exoneration

Let's say you are a parent, and your son breaks a window in your house. You had warned him about playing ball in the house before, but he just ignored the warnings, thinking that the chances of breaking a window were so slight that he would go ahead and do it anyway. However, as slim as those chances may have been, it happened. Your son is now regretful and as sorry about it as he can be. Of course, as a loving parent, you forgive him. You may be annoyed that he disobeyed you, but you have no intention of holding it over his head forever.

Your son is now forgiven, but is the window still broken? Yes. Has your son fully learned his lesson for his transgression? No, not until he pays for the broken window. Though you have forgiven him, as a parent who cares about your son's sense of responsibility, the transgression cannot be completely exonerated. There must still be a price paid for disobedience. This is necessary for your son if he is to become a man of solid character. He can't possibly afford the monetary cost of the window. But allowing him to get away with it without consequences would be irresponsible of you as a parent.

Though the price was much higher than that of a window, this is what God did for Adam and Eve. He removed them from the perfection of Eden and made them pay a heavy penalty for their transgression. They were fairly warned but chose to disobey. God forgave them, but the law was still broken. The problem: the price of their broken window (broken communion with God) was so high that no man could pay it. Only God Himself had that ability.

However, so great was God's love for them that He provided a temporary fix for that window of communion in the form of a substitutionary sacrifice through which forgiveness was achieved—sort of like trying to glue the shards of glass back together until a new, permanent window could be installed. The view of God is now distorted and fuzzy. Far from perfect, it is better than no window at all. The good news is that the Window Installer has come and measured for the new pane; when He left, He sent the Holy Spirit to improve the view in the old pane, and He is now in the process of making the new pane perfect for those who choose to have faith in His work. We are currently looking forward to the day that the perfect view (perfect communion with God—beatific vision) is fully restored. (More on that later)

Blood is the Key

For now, the critical thing to know is that blood, without fail, is *the* essential element in all covenants (contractual agreements) between God and man.

> *After the Great Flood, when God made a covenant with His creation (that He would never again curse the ground or destroy every living thing with water), Noah, as part of that creation, made an offering of "every clean animal and every clean bird..." Gen. 8:20*

When God promised Abram an heir and innumerable descendants, in order to seal the covenant, God Himself performed the binding ceremony among the sacrificed animals (Gen. 15). (This covenant was quite unique and warrants your further study! In essence, God was foretelling the sacrifice of the Messiah as He took this oath upon Himself in place of Abram.)

Yet again, when Abram received his new name (Abraham) from God, and the covenant of circumcision was prescribed, the blood from the very act of circumcising his whole household became the sealing agent in that covenant (Gen. 17).

Why Did Jesus Have to Die?

The examples are numerous. Suffice it to say, any time there is a contractual agreement, either established by God to man or established by man to God, blood acts as the seal of that agreement.

This brings us to, perhaps, the most unique sacrifice ever recorded in the Old Testament. Genesis 15:6 records that Abraham (Abram at the time) believed God, and God "accounted it to him for righteousness." Obviously, Abraham's faith was great. However, that faith had yet to be thoroughly tested. By the time we get to chapter 22, God remedies that situation in the form of a request that, understandably, must have baffled Abraham:

> "Now it came to pass after these things that God tested Abraham, and said to him, 'Abraham!'
>
> "And he said, 'Here I am.'
>
> "Then He said, 'Take now your son, your only son Isaac, whom you love, and go to the land of Moriah, and offer him there as a burnt offering on one of the mountains of which I shall tell you.'" Gen. 22:1-2

Abraham had waited so long for this son. This was the son of promise—the very son through whom God had promised to make his descendants as numerous as the stars in the sky. And now that he finally had him, God was asking for his life to be offered as a sacrifice? Just for a moment, put yourself in Abraham's sandals. For most, if not all of us who have children, there is no question whether or not an argument with God would ensue. I consider myself a man of great faith. God has asked hard things of me in the past, and I have obeyed without question. However, I must admit, I cannot imagine a scenario in which I would sacrifice my own child without, at least, my begging God to take me instead! So, what did Abraham do?

> "So Abraham rose early in the morning and saddled his donkey, and took two of his young men with him, and Isaac his son; and he split the wood for the burnt offering, and arose and went to the place of which God had told him." Gen. 22:3

There was no argument, begging, or pleading; no deal making; and no questions. Many theologians, pastors, and Bible teachers have put forth theories on Abraham's inner turmoil and his motivations for his unquestioning obedience to God in this unthinkable situation. However, the only explanation that makes any sense is the one that had endeared him to God in the first place: unwavering faith. Abraham knew that the God who made the heavens and the earth would make a way. Any speculation that he thought God would bring Isaac back to life, that God would change His mind, or that God would provide a substitute makes for interesting conversation, but there is really no way to know his mind.

I believe the salient point here, one that transcends the "what ifs" of our worldly thinking, is that no matter what it is that God asks of us—be it money, time, effort, our thoughts, or even our children—if we offer it in faith, freely and without reservation, God will honor it. I believe that Abraham had a firm understanding of his own place in the hierarchy of his existence. By this, I mean to say that everything belonged to God in Abraham's view of faith. He, as a mere grain of sand on the beach of humanity, had absolutely no right to question the God who could snuff it all out in an instant. This God, who had been good to him in all things and promised him

Why Did Jesus Have to Die?

descendants as numerous as the stars, would keep His promises and honor the sacrifice when given in pure faith. In the end, this is precisely what God did:

> "And Abraham stretched out his hand and took the knife to slay his son. But the Angel of the LORD called to him from Heaven and said, 'Abraham, Abraham!'
>
> "So he said, 'Here I am.'
>
> "And He said, 'Do not lay your hand on the lad, or do anything to him; for now I know that you fear God, since you have not withheld your son, your only son, from Me.'" Gen. 22:10-12

Note: This passage of Scripture says, "...*the Angel of the LORD*...." When you see "*Angel of the LORD,*" this is known as a *Christophany*—an Old Testament appearance of Christ.

Discussion Questions

1. Putting yourself in the place of Adam or Eve, having just lost that beatific vision of God, what kind of emotions do you think they were feeling?

2. Are the concepts of forgiveness vs. exoneration, using the parental model, helpful in understanding God's response to sin? If not, how would you present it?

3. Is your faith strong enough that you would have done what God asked of Abraham without argument? (As stated above, the author has already admitted to his own troubles answering this question!)

Chapter Three

A Substitute is Provided

Continuing from Chapter 2, we pick up the story of Abraham's test of faith on Mount Moriah. The *"Angel of the LORD"* (Christ) had just stayed his hand from slaying Isaac.

> *"Then Abraham lifted his eyes and looked, and there behind him was a ram caught in a thicket by its horns. So Abraham went and took the ram, and offered it up for a burnt offering instead of his son. And Abraham called the name of the place, The-LORD-Will-Provide; as it is said to this day, 'In the Mount of the LORD it shall be provided.'"* Gen. 22:13-14

Every book of the Old Testament is said to point to Christ. However, the above verses not only point to Christ (the ram being symbolic of Christ in this story), but also to His destiny as a substitutionary sacrifice. Though many examples in the Old Testament foreshadow the future work of Christ, the above verses are as clear as any could be. And while we could explore these to a great degree, they would take us off our study path. The substitutionary nature of the sacrifice is the concept at hand.

Why Did Jesus Have to Die?

As we travel forward in time to where the Levitical Laws were put in place for the nation of Israel and guided their everyday living, we see that, no matter what the sin, and even where there is no apparent sin but what is inherent to fallen man, blood sacrifice is the central mechanism of atonement. Sins that would serve to severely infect the morality of the nation as a whole (such as murder, adultery, and homosexuality) were dealt with swiftly, and no sacrificial atonement was prescribed. In those cases, the wrongdoer's very life was forfeit. However, the day-to-day offenses to the Law were to be atoned for through the sacrifices of various animals. In most cases, the degree of the offense dictated the value of the sacrificed animal. (These should obviously not be confused with the grain offerings prescribed in Leviticus, chapter 2.)

There was also another vital requirement for these sacrifices, especially the ones meant to cover the greater degrees of sin; they were to be *"without blemish."* In chapter 1 of Leviticus, God Himself gave the prescription for the burnt offerings:

> *"If his offering is a burnt sacrifice of the herd, let him offer* **a male without blemish;** *he shall offer it of his own free will at the door of the Tabernacle of meeting before the LORD. Then he shall put his hand on the head of the burnt offering,* **and it will be accepted on his behalf to make atonement for him."** vs. 3-4

The same requirement is prescribed for the sacrificial animals as sin offerings, as well as peace offerings, in chapters 3 and 4. In fact, in chapters 1, 3, and 4, the words *"without blemish"* appear eight times.

In essence, all of these sacrifices were substitutionary in nature. God, in His mercy, made allowances in the Law, allowing His people to atone for their sins with the blood of animals as substitutions

A Substitute is Provided

for their own blood. An animal died in place of Adam and Eve to cover (literally) their sin. As a reward to Abraham for his great faith, God provided a substitute sacrifice instead of Isaac. When the Angel of Death passed over Egypt, God allowed for the substitutionary blood of lambs on the doorposts of their houses to protect against the death penalty on all the firstborns of the land.

The Temporary (single-use) Nature of Sacrificial Atonement in the Law

> **Note 1**: I would like to clear up any misunderstanding of what "temporary (single-use)" means. When I say "temporary," it has to do with the fact that man is naturally bent toward sin, and he will naturally keep sinning. Therefore, he will have to keep repeating the process of atonement. First, the specific sins atoned for through those animal sacrifices were forgiven forever. Second, as discussed earlier, there is a difference between forgiveness and exoneration. While *specific* sins could be forgiven, the sacrificial system of the Levitical Laws could never lead to complete exoneration of *all* sins.
>
> **Note 2**: It is essential to remember that any sacrifices, unto themselves, were of no use as atoning mechanisms if they were not done in faith. Faith is always the oil that makes the mechanism work. Certainly, when a man brought his sacrifice to the altar, the very act of doing so would inherently require some measure of faith in God that his sins would be forgiven. However, there was also a social expectancy involved. The man's neighbors would be aware if the man did not make a sacrifice as they did themselves. If the man brought the sacrifice out of his perceived social obligations, but without faith, his neighbors may honor his sacrifice, but not God.

The people of Israel, it seems, would have had to be almost constantly at the Tabernacle atoning for their sins. This in itself would have served to deter the Israelites from sin. Putting yourself in their place, if you were a cattle rancher and every time you sinned, you had to go to church and offer up the absolute best of your herd, how often would you be there? No matter how many cattle I had to begin with, by the end of the year, I might not have many cattle remaining in my fields! Yet, this is precisely what the Israelites had to do. Over and over, even the best among them were required to make offerings for the same repeated sins, new sins, and even sins they may not have recognized as sins.

The reason for this goes back, once again, to Eden. The curse pronounced at the Fall was not only on man but all creation. Though the Law prescribed a sacrifice "without blemish," we know that, no matter how perfect an animal may look, it is inherently flawed due to the degradation of everything in this world brought on by the pervasive taint of sin. If we pick a beautiful orange that looks absolutely "perfect," we know it will eventually rot. If a master carpenter builds a "perfect" table, he knows it is not truly perfect because it will eventually break down with age.

The Word of God, and as a result of the Fall, the 2nd Law of Thermodynamics (specifically, the Law of Entropy), informs us that everything in our universe has a shelf-life and will eventually succumb to the ravages of time. Therefore, when an animal "without blemish" was offered as an atonement for sin, the atonement was only temporary because the blemish, though not apparent visually, was inherent due to the curse of the Fall in Eden. Thus, only a **Truly Perfect Substitutionary Blood Sacrifice** would make for an ***eternally binding atonement***.

Discussion Questions

1. Have you ever truly thought out the substitutionary nature of the Old Testament sacrifices? Does that heighten your awareness of your own sin?

A Substitute is Provided

2. What does the provision of a substitutionary sacrificial system tell you about the nature of God?

3. Sacrifices given out of obligation instead of faith were of no use. Have you ever tithed or given an offering out of obligation rather than the joy that comes from faith?

Chapter Four

Why Did Jesus Have to Die? Part 2

The Perfection of Christ

Though it took a while to get to this point, the concepts covered so far needed firm establishment to truly understand the question, "Why did Jesus have to die?"

- We now understand that, though man tends to concern himself mainly with physical death, spiritual death (the loss of perfect communion and relationship with God) is the real problem that must be overcome.

- We now understand the importance of blood as the binding agent for any covenant made with God.

- We now understand the substitutionary nature of the prescribed sacrifices of the Levitical Laws and that the blood of those animals served only as a temporary (single-use) atonement because those animals were inherently tainted by sin as a result of the Fall of Man in Eden.

- Thus, a *Truly Perfect Substitutionary Blood Sacrifice* is needed to affect a permanent, all-encompassing atonement for man's specific and inherent sin. Also, man must have an unfettered ability to choose whether to place his faith in that *Truly Perfect Substitutionary Blood Sacrifice*.

What are the requirements of a *Truly Perfect Substitutionary Blood Sacrifice*?

1. The Sacrifice must be born **without the sin nature** inherent in Adam's seed. According to Genesis 3:15, the Messiah would be of a woman's seed. This means two things: First, the Sacrifice would be a **Person, not an animal.** Second, **for this Messiah to be born without the seed of a man, a virgin birth was necessary**.

2. The Sacrifice must strictly follow every single one of the Mosaic/Levitical Laws, **living a life free of any sin that would negate His perfection**.

3. The Sacrifice must be **willing** to stand in as a Substitutionary Blood Sacrifice for the sins of man and the curse brought on through Adam.

4. The Sacrifice must be God in human form. Since God alone is perfect, and all men are sinful, **the Sacrifice must be a God-man**.

5. This Perfect Sacrifice must conceal His full glory as God in the flesh. If He overwhelmed humanity with His full glory, He would leave man with no choice but to accept Him for who He is. This would negate

man's free will. Each man is responsible for his own sin. Therefore, **each man/woman must be free to choose whether or not to put his/her faith in this Perfect Sacrifice as Messiah.**

Thus, based on the above requirements, Jesus of Nazareth is the only Person in the history of the world who has fulfilled all these requirements. There is absolutely no need to look any further. Not only did He fulfill those specific requirements, but He fulfilled around 300 specific prophecies about the Messiah recorded in the Old Testament. Therefore, **Jesus of Nazareth was and is the *Truly Perfect Substitutionary Blood Sacrifice*.** He is the God-man—the Messiah—who alone was able to affect an eternally binding atonement for the world's sin problem. All that is needed is for each person to put their faith in Jesus' sacrifice to atone for their sin. Moreover, faith in Jesus for atonement results in an eventual full exoneration for sin, just as if no sin were ever committed. Also, through His finished work as the Perfect Sacrifice, He achieved an eternal atonement for all of creation, reversing the curse of the Fall, and fully redeemable at a time of His choosing (In part, during the Millennial Reign; and in whole, in the New Jerusalem).

Discussion Questions

1. Other than the 4 bullet points of things we can now understand to answer the question, "Why Did Jesus Have to Die?" have you come to understand any other truths through this study so far? If so, what?

2. Given the 5 requirements of a Truly Perfect Substitutionary Blood Sacrifice listed above, do any stand out to you? If so, why?

3. Read Isaiah 53 and, as a group or by yourself, count how many prophecies Jesus fulfilled in that single passage.

Chapter Five

What Did Jesus' Sacrifice Accomplish?

Several words are often used to describe what was accomplished by Jesus' sacrifice. On the surface, they may seem like different words that boil down to the same meaning. However, as we will see, the precise implications of these words describe separate and distinct facets of Jesus' accomplishment. We will briefly go through the most often used of these theologically based words for clarification. Though many theologians have defined these words, I believe Charles C. Ryrie relates them in the most straightforward and understandable way in his widely used and respected textbook, *Basic Theology* (Moody Press; Chicago, Ill.; ©1999).

Jesus' Sacrifice was…
1. A Substitution for Sinners

"Substitutionary or vicarious atonement simply means that Christ suffered as a substitute for us, that is, instead of us, resulting in the advantage to us of paying for our sins.

"Man could atone for his sins personally only if he could suffer eternally the penalty that sin incurred. Man, of course, could never do this, so in His love and compassion, God stepped into a hopeless situation and provided a Vicar in Jesus Christ who did provide an eternal satisfaction for sin." (p. 329)

2. A Redemption in Relation to Sin

"Redemption means liberation because of a payment made. To believers the concept has a special significance since the payment was the death of the Lord Himself." (p. 334)

3. A Reconciliation in Relation to the World

"Reconciliation means a change of relationship from hostility to harmony and peace between two parties. People can be reconciled to each other (Matt. 5:24, *diallasso*; 1 Cor. 7:11, *katallasso*), and people have been reconciled to God (Rom. 5:1-11; 2 Cor. 5:18-21, *katallasso*; Eph. 2:16; Col. 1:20, *apokatallasso*)." (p. 336)

4. A Propitiation in Relation to God

"Propitiation means the turning away of wrath by an offering. In relation to soteriology, propitiation means placating or satisfying the wrath of God by the atoning sacrifice of Christ." (p. 339)

Because of the above, when a person puts his or her faith in the sacrifice of Christ, each believer personally experiences some significant results. Again, Charles C. Ryrie's *Basic Theology* is most helpful in defining these.

Faith in Jesus' Sacrifice Results in...

1. Justification

"Justification is not only one of the great benefits of the death of Christ but is also a cardinal doctrine of

Christianity because it distinguishes it as a religion of grace and faith. And grace and faith are the cornerstones of the doctrine of justification.

A. The Meaning of Justification

"To justify means to declare righteous. Both the Hebrew (sadaq) and the Greek (dikaioo) words mean to announce or pronounce a favorable verdict, to declare righteous. The concept does not mean to make righteous, but to announce righteousness. It is a courtroom concept, so that to justify is to give a verdict of righteous. Notice the contrast between to justify and to condemn in Deuteronomy 25:1; 1 Kings 8:32; and Proverbs 17:15. Just as announcing condemnation does not make a person wicked, neither does justification make a person righteous. Condemning or justifying announces the true and actual state of the person. The wicked person is already wicked when the verdict of condemnation is pronounced. Likewise, the righteous person is already righteous when the verdict of justification is announced." (p. 343)

2. The Judgment of the Sin Nature

"A second very important benefit of the death of Christ relates His death to the judgment of the believer's sin nature (Rom. 6:1-14). Justification, we saw, will be seen in a life of holiness; and the basis for that life of holiness, like the basis for justification, is the death of Christ.

"In the preceding chapter Paul used that startling phrase, 'the gift of righteousness' (5:17). This raises the question of 6:1. If righteousness is a gift, then would it not be better to continue in sin in order that grace may increasingly be seen? If salvation were by works, this question would never be raised, since one would have to keep on doing good works in order to merit salvation. But if salvation is by grace, then cannot one sin as much as he pleases, and will this not actually display grace all the more? Paul answers the question with an emphatic no. He gives two reasons that the justified person will not continue in sin."

First, the judgment frees us from the domain of sin (Rom. 6:2-10). Second, the judgment frees us from the dominion of sin (Rom. 6:11-14). (pp. 345-47; final statements paraphrased)

3. The Basis for the Believer's Family Fellowship

"No passage is more basic for understanding the believer's family fellowship than 1 John 1:5-10. In it, John lays down vital principles for daily Christian living, and this fellowship is based on the death of Christ (v. 7). Thus, another benefit of His death is that it provides for enjoyment of fellowship within the family of God." (p. 347)

4. Adoption

"Adoption is the act of God that places the believer in His family as an adult. In contrast, being born again emphasizes the idea of coming into God's family as a babe with the attendant need for growth and development (John 1:12; 3:3). But adoption teaches the ideas of adulthood and full privileges in the family of God. Concomitant with adoption is the divesting of all relationships and responsibilities of the previous family relationship. Both being adopted and being born occur at the moment of saving faith, but they indicate different aspects of our relation to the family of God." (p 352)

[There is one more point which could be spelled out in lay terms rather than in more theological terms, which tends to muddle the impact of this truth. My esteemed colleague, Charles C. Ryrie, is without peer as a theologian. However, his brilliant eloquence can overshadow the simpler facets of this point.]

5. Fulfillment of the Law

As Jesus lived out the perfect life, fulfilling every single facet of the Levitical Law, both in deed and intention, He was able to do what was impossible for anyone else in history! Thus, having done that, the Law has become something different than before. Let's view it as a checklist of sorts. Before Jesus came, it was a checklist of things to be accomplished, but there was no one who could check off even one of those items. But, when Jesus came, He was able to check off everything, signing off with His own precious blood!

However, it is also important to understand that though Jesus fulfilled the 613 individual laws, that doesn't mean that none of the laws still apply. Obviously, murder, theft, lying, adultery, and the rest of the Ten Commandments are still valuable guidelines for all of mankind to follow. And, as Jesus alluded to, the two greatest commandments boil down to: 1. Love God with all your being, and 2. Love your neighbor as yourself.

Nevertheless, many of the dietary laws, though following them may have great health benefits, are no longer considered sins if they are not followed. For example, it was against the Law to eat or even touch pork. But God illustrated a change through Peter's vision of all the unclean animals in Acts 10. Though this vision applied to salvation available to the Gentiles, it also applies to dietary laws. Those laws were meant to set God's people, Israel, apart from the heathen nations. What

Jesus accomplished served to set apart His people, both Jew and Gentile, in a more important, spiritual way. And, while bacon may not be the healthiest thing for me to eat, God does not condemn me for eating it. For this, I am so very thankful to God! At any rate, following the Law is a good idea and can lead to a healthier life, but if you rely on the Law for your salvation, you exchange what Jesus did for what you can do. There is simply no comparison!

I want to add one more caveat to the above. If you believe or feel that eating certain things, worshiping on certain days, or anything else in the Law is sin, then for you it is sin. I have friends who believe eating pork is against God's Law. I do not, especially for a Gentile. However, we each have to come to a settlement within, aligning our minds and spirits with the Holy Spirit within. Therefore, if my eating bacon bothers a brother or sister in Christ who believes it is sin, I should not eat it and cause them to stumble. (1 Cor. 8) We each have to *"work out (y)our own salvation with fear and trembling."* (Phil. 2:12)

Discussion Questions

1. Did any of the definitions for substitution, redemption, reconciliation, and propitiation make an impression on you or help you better understand Jesus' sacrifice?

2. Same question for the results of Jesus' sacrifice.

3. Do you ever feel as though your inability to be perfect will negate Jesus' grace? If so, where do you think those feelings come from?

Chapter Six

The Process of Salvation; Part 1

Every believer in Christ has a story, a testimony, of how they received the greatest gift that God could give. Though salvation comes to everyone in different and unique ways, there is a basic process, an order, in which salvation transpires. Some elements of a person's salvation were in place before the fact; others happen simultaneously to the fact; others happen after the fact on a long-term basis; and others will occur at the grand culmination of all things—at the edge of a new, eternal existence on which our finite minds can only speculate. As so often happens, many debates and arguments have been made over the specifics of these elements, but the order in which they occur tends to find more agreement. In this section, we will discuss them in that order.

First: Election

Perhaps the most contentious of debates within the Body of Christ regarding the salvation process, the doctrine of election has been the source of many divisions within the Church. The argument does not center around whether or not there is such a doctrine; Scripture clearly addresses it as such. Rather, the debate is centered more on the mechanics of the doctrine—how it works. As we will see, this element of the process of salvation must be the first element discussed due to the nature of its implications. First things first, the best example of the doctrine's Scriptural basis is found in chapter 1 of Paul's epistle to the Ephesians:

> (3) "Blessed be the God and Father of our Lord Jesus Christ, who has blessed us with every spiritual blessing in the heavenly places in Christ, (4) **just as He chose us in Him before the foundation of the world**, that we should be holy and without blame before Him in love, (5) **having predestined us to adoption as sons by Jesus Christ Himself, according to the good pleasure of His will**, (6) to the praise of the glory of His grace, by which He made us accepted in the Beloved.

> (7) "In Him we have redemption through His blood, the forgiveness of sins, according to the riches of His grace (8) which He made to abound toward us in all wisdom and prudence, (9) having made known to us the mystery of His will, according to His good pleasure which He purposed in Himself, (10) that in the dispensation of the fullness of the times He might gather together in one all things in Christ, both which are in Heaven and which are on earth—in Him. (11) **In Him also we have obtained an inheritance, being predestined according to the purpose of Him who works all things according to the council of His will**, (12) that we who trusted in Christ should be to the praise of His glory.

> *(13) "In Him you also trusted, after you heard the word of truth, the gospel of your salvation; in whom also, having believed, you were sealed with the Holy Spirit of promise, (14) who is the guarantee of our inheritance until the redemption of the purchased possession, to the praise of His glory."* (Emphasis added)

These verses obviously cover much theological ground on the subject of salvation. However, regarding the doctrine of election, verses 4, 5, and 11 are the most informative. In fact, based on those verses, the best definition for election is one taken directly from the Scriptures. Before defining the doctrine of election, it is crucial to have a solid basis in Scripture on which to establish that definition. Thus, election means:

By His grace, God chose us (believers) before He laid the foundations of the world; He chose to adopt us as His sons and daughters according to the pleasure of His good will; and that, being predestined for His grace, we have an inheritance, which is guaranteed by the seal of the Holy Spirit, and which will be fully redeemed in the fullness of time when Christ gathers all things unto Himself to God's glory.
(My own definition, paraphrased from Scripture)

Therefore, given the implications of our predestined salvation, this element in the process of salvation had to be dealt with first. The arguments surround the exact extent of that predestination in juxtaposition with man's free will. Though there are several opinions on the subject, they all boil down to two definable camps of thought: Calvinism and Arminianism.

Calvinist View

The Calvinist views, as they pertain to the subject of election, are generally spelled out in what are popularly referred to as the "five points of Calvinism." These five distinctives, though not directly authored by John Calvin (1509-1564), are the product of the Synod of Dort (1619). They are particularly useful in pointing out the differences between Calvinist and Arminian theologies. As per this study, these five points will serve to give you a good perspective of the basis on which the Calvinists build their thoughts on the doctrine of election. In *The Moody Handbook of Theology*, Paul Enns provides those five points as follows:

Five Points of Calvinism

Doctrine	Explanation
Total Depravity	As a result of Adam's Fall, the entire human race is affected; all humanity is dead in trespasses and sin. Man is unable to save himself.
Unconditional Election	Because man is dead in sin, he is unable to initiate response to God; therefore, in eternity past God elected certain people to salvation. Election and predestination are unconditional; they are not based on man's response.
Limited Atonement	Because God determined that certain ones should be saved as a result of God's unconditional election, He determined that Christ should die for the elect. All whom God has elected and Christ died for will be saved.
Irresistible Grace	Those whom God elected and Christ died for, God draws to Himself through irresistible grace. God makes man willing to come to Him. When God calls, man responds.
Perseverance of the Saints	The precise ones God has elected and drawn to Himself through the Holy Spirit will persevere in faith. None whom God has elected will be lost; they are eternally secure

(Moody Press; Moody Bible Institute; Chicago, Ill.; ©1989; p. 480)

Arminian View

For the purpose of direct comparison, we will now look at the Arminian view. Like Calvin, Jacobus Arminius (1560-1609) was a renowned theologian during the Reformation. *The Moody Handbook of Theology* is of good use here as well. In it, Paul Enns spells out the Arminian view in the same fashion as he did for the five points of Calvinism above:

Arminian Doctrine (The Remonstrance)

Doctrine	Explanation
Election Based on Knowledge	God elected those whom He knew would of their own free will believe in Christ and persevere in the faith.
Unlimited Atonement	In His atonement, Christ provided redemption for all mankind, making all mankind savable. Christ's atonement becomes effective only in those who believe.
Natural Inability	Man cannot save himself; the Holy Spirit must affect the new birth.
Prevenient Grace	Preparatory work of the Holy Spirit enables the believer to respond to the Gospel and cooperate with God in salvation.
Conditional Perseverance	Believers have been empowered to live a victorious life, but they are capable of turning from grace and losing their salvation.

(Moody Press; Moody Bible Institute; Chicago, Ill.; ©1989; p. 495)

As the charts above show, there is ample room for disagreement within the Body of Christ on this difficult doctrine. The fact is, as hard as it may be to understand, the doctrine of election exists. Calvin and Arminius were both great men of faith who felt strongly about their respective positions on the subject. However, as the charts also indicate, they represent the extreme ends of this field of thought.

That being said, there are problems on both sides. The Calvinist's view is rigidly hard-lined and tends to make the act of salvation a one-sided affair. His view seems to ignore man's free will and limits the scope of God's loving offer of salvation to only those whom He chose. The Arminian view tends to limit God's ability to keep those He has saved. His "conditional perseverance" stance draws an arbitrary line that intimates that, though the regenerate man will still struggle with sin, there is some undefined tipping point that, if crossed, will result in a loss of salvation. Therefore, he makes salvation a works-based endeavor. As with all arguments involving biblical doctrines, the truth lies in the Scriptures. After all, Scripture is the best interpreter of Scripture.

The plain reading of Ephesians 1:3-12 (cited above) states that all believers are predestined to their salvation. The point of argument seems to revolve around the accusations leveled at the Calvinists that, given that some are predestined to Heaven, the Calvinistic model says that God has, therefore, predestined others to Hell. This, from the Arminian standpoint, makes free will of no consequence. What, then, do other Scriptures have to say on the matter? If this is the proper view of Scripture, we expect that other Scriptures will bear it out.

John 6:37 states, **"All that the Father gives Me will come to Me,** *and the one who comes to Me* **I will by no means cast out."**

Jesus says in John 6:44, **"No one can come to Me unless the Father who sent Me draws him;** *and I will raise him up at the last day."* (Repeated in v. 65)

In John 15:16, Jesus states, **"You did not choose Me, but I chose you and appointed you** *that you should go and bear fruit, and that* **your fruit should remain,** *that whatever you ask the Father in My name He may give you."*

The Process of Salvation; Part 1

Acts 13:48 says, *"Now when the Gentiles heard this, they were glad and glorified the word of the Lord.* **And as many as had been appointed to eternal life believed.***"*

As we can see, Scripture agrees on the question of predestination. Like it or not (and a great many do not), the statements of Jesus Himself back up the Calvinist view (though, when taken to extremes, can lead to heretical "super-grace" teachings). However, the question remains; has God then predestined others to Hell?

The Arminian view (though, when taken to extremes, has led to heretical liberalism) contends that all are savable and anyone can choose to follow Christ. Are there, then, Scriptures to back up that assertion? The answer is yes. The following verses seem to point in that direction:

2 Peter 3:9 states, *"The Lord is not slack concerning His promise, as some count slackness, but is longsuffering toward us,* **not willing that any should perish but that all should come to repentance.***"*

1 Timothy 2:3-4 says, *"For this is good and acceptable in the sight of God our Savior,* **who desires all men to be saved and to come to the knowledge of the truth.***"*

In Matthew 11:28, Jesus, without restriction, says, *"Come to Me* **all** *you who labor and are heavy laden, and I will give you rest."*

From these verses, it is clear that the call to salvation is for "all," not just those who are specially chosen. And, if all could not be saved, that call would be insincere—a ludicrous line of thought that questions God's loving nature. So, what is the answer? Who is correct, the Calvinist or the Arminian? Our perspectives must be tempered by humility and the knowledge that we, as fallen beings, are very capable of error. ***If two opposing*** *views seem to agree with Scripture, our understanding of Scripture* (and, by extension, our understanding of God's nature) *is at fault, not the Scripture itself.*

The Thornton Understanding of the Doctrine of Election

If God is who He says He is, then in Him alone (due to His perfections: omniscience, omnipresence, and omnipotence), both views, minus some minor details, can be correct. In the timelessness of eternity past, when God thought to create this world and all the creatures that would inhabit it, because of who He is, it would have been outside His very nature not to see the end from the beginning. You see, for God, eternity past, present, and future are all one singularity because, for Him, there is no time but the time He created—this thing to which we humans are bound.

In God's unbridled creativity, He could choose any string of possibilities He wished. Because He is love exemplified, He chose to give us free will and desired us to return His love of our own accord. However, because He is also justice personified and knew that we would misuse our free will, He set forth a plan to give us the clearest choice possible: Follow Him and share eternity with Him in love, or reject His offer and separate ourselves from Him forever. Due to His infinite foresight and omniscience, how could He *not* know who would and would not choose to follow or reject? Therefore, in this string of possibilities that He chose—this thing we call human existence, past, present, and future—the ones who would use their free will to follow Him were, are, and will be His elect.

In this view, all are savable. The call to salvation is universal in its scope. However, only the elect are the ones who choose to heed that call. Because of God's capacity to love, He wants all to accept Him and live forever. Because of God's justice, He gives all the choice but allows them to choose wrongly. While the Bible speaks of those elect who were predestined to life, it never says that all the rest were predestined to death and separation from God. It only says that those who reject His offer will suffer from that choice. **While God delights in our choice to follow Him, He never revels in our choice not to do so.**

In essence, the doctrine of election should not be argued over as a negative but embraced as a positive. For God has chosen us to do good works. In so doing, He has provided us a way to enjoy a degree of ownership in our salvation—to work for His Kingdom. **He did not save us *because* of our good works, but He saved us *to do* good works, thereby becoming a prism through which the pure light of His Holy Spirit can shine in myriad colors as a beacon for the lost.**

Discussion Questions

1. Does the fact that God chose you before this world was ever even created make you feel more like He flipped a cosmic coin and you happened to win, or does it make you feel that you have been given a sense of ownership in your salvation since you used your free will to follow Him?

2. After hearing the tenets of Calvinism and Arminianism, do you fall in one camp more than the other, or do you see it closer to the author's view (the "Thornton" view as spelled out above)?

3. Do you view this argument over election as a distraction from the Church's true calling: sharing the Gospel and making disciples?

Chapter Seven

The Process of Salvation; Part 2

The doctrine of election discussed in the previous chapter took a lot of time to discuss properly due to its intricacies. As you will soon see, the views described there inform our upcoming discussions. Now, we can move on to the second step in the process of salvation.

Second: Effectual Calling, Prevenient Grace, or General Grace

Depending on the camp with which you identify (Calvinist or Arminian), these three terms mean relatively the same thing. The difference lies in who receives the benefit. The Calvinist will use the term "**effectual calling**" to describe that special act of the Holy Spirit, whereby He undoes the Fall in the heart of only the elect, effectively opening their eyes to the truth of the Gospel. In this Calvinistic viewpoint, the affected elect will have no choice but to believe and, therefore, be regenerated and receive their foreordained salvation. In this view, the willpower of the elect is completely unable to overcome the calling.

However, the Arminian will use the term "**prevenient grace**" to describe much the same thing. This term also carries the connotation of a subtle wooing or drawing over time by the Holy Spirit to bring one to that point of decision. If they choose salvation, they become a member of the elect; If they choose to stay dead in their sins, they are lost. In this view, each person must choose to accept or reject the call.

Therefore, whether **effectual calling** or **prevenient grace**, the terms may be defined as a special calling by the Holy Spirit to an unbeliever prior to rejection of, or saving faith in, Jesus Christ. In other words, the wooing of the Holy Spirit readies the unbelieving heart for planting the seeds of faith. How many Christians have testified that they were blind but suddenly could see? However, though that true sight may have come suddenly, were there not occurrences prior to this that put them on the road toward faith? The question then becomes, when did the call go out?

I can only testify to my experiences. I once reveled in my life of sin. I was perfectly content. Then, things happened in my life which caused me to question that life. I realized I was no longer content and felt a great void in my heart. This brought on a desire to search for the answers to those questions for which a seeking and sin-sick heart strives to answer. Finally, I heard one thing in a church service—nothing of any real significance that would result in great numbers of people rushing to the altar—which, for reasons I would find hard to describe, caused a sudden heartbreak and a pang of hunger to fill that aching void with God. Personally, I would call that the **effectual calling**.

So, based on my personal experience, how should I amend the definition of this grace prior to salvation? How far back did that call begin? When I was 12 years old, I was riding with a neighbor on a 3-wheeler motorcycle down a severely pot-holed road. My neighbor lost control, and the 3-wheeler shot into the ditch and toward a barbed wire fence. My neighbor managed to jump, but I was hurtled into the fence, between the two top wires. I slid on my neck between two tight strands of wire with its razor-sharp barbs before slamming my head into a post and landing on the other side. By all accounts, I should have been beheaded. If not, I should have had my throat cut severely enough to open my jugular and bleed to death. However, though I had dozens of definable gashes across my neck, which were millimeters from the necessary depth to kill me, I came out of it with a shredded shirt, a bloody neck, and a bump on my head. Was that not an act of **general grace** that allowed me to live long enough to accept Christ's offer of salvation?

The point is, I believe that to live any life in which, at some point, you hear the Gospel and make your choice is a life filled with that special grace that allowed you that choice. I believe that the moment when the Holy Spirit suddenly opens your heart to the truth of the Gospel is a special act of the Spirit, which comes only after God has orchestrated your life so that you begin searching for truth. The wooing is a long-term operation; the revealing comes at the right time when you are genuinely ready to make a decision, and then, either life or death results from that decision. Therefore, I would say that God extends a **general grace** to all. He gifts **prevenient grace** which draws all toward His truth. And, He wants all to heed His call, making their personal decision to accept His gift, thereby making that **call effectual**. If not, each person has the ability—free will—to ignore the call of the Holy Spirit.

Third: Faith, the Indwelling of the Holy Spirit, and Regeneration

Faith, the indwelling of the Holy Spirit, and regeneration can be rightly seen as simultaneous occurrences. However, each element must also be present, in turn, for the next to occur. Faith must be present for the Holy Spirit to indwell the believer, and the Holy Spirit affects the regeneration of the newly reborn. Therefore, either each comes in turn, separated by some tiny unit of time, or all three come at once, working as a single unit to affect the rebirth. Nonetheless, we will define each element in turn.

Faith

Once the calling of the Holy Spirit is done, and one has his eyes opened to the truth of the Gospel, a decision must be made—to either answer the call or ignore it. **The decision to follow Christ must be made in faith.** Therefore, faith is attained somewhere between the opening of the spiritual eyes and heart and the decision being made. As discussed earlier, this element is the basis for salvation (Eph. 2:8). **Good works, no matter how altruistic and selfless they may be, are utterly useless without faith.**

The Indwelling of the Holy Spirit

The presence of faith makes possible the indwelling of the Holy Spirit. Make no mistake, this is God, the Holy Spirit—the third Person of the Triune Godhead—taking up permanent residence within the receiver's being. He immediately fills the void (the proverbial "God-shaped hole") within the receiver's heart. This is also known as the "baptism of the Holy Spirit." The indwelling of the Holy Spirit is a once-and-for-all occurrence. Once there, the Holy Spirit will never leave. In fact, He places a seal on the new believer (Eph. 4:30), which cannot be removed, and preserves the believer until the day of final redemption. (2 Cor. 1:22)

Regeneration

This is the point at which the believer becomes a "new creature." (2 Cor. 5:17). Faith was a choice made by the seeker to place trust in Jesus and His atoning sacrifice, leading to an invitation—an open door—for the Holy Spirit to take up permanent residence (John 14:17) within the seeker. These were actions initiated by the seeker. On the other hand, regeneration is an action initiated by God, whereby the seeker becomes a fully vested child of God. The adoption into the family of God is now complete. In conjunction with faith (the believer's trust in Jesus' sacrifice as sufficient for atonement) and with the permanent seal of the Holy Spirit in place, regeneration is a new and permanent state of existence. The old carnal nature is now replaced by the "new creature." Where the carnal man of before was born of flesh (with the sin nature from the seed of Adam), the "new creature" is born of the Spirit so that the broken communion of the Fall begins to be reversed, and access to God the Holy Spirit is now available. However, although spiritual access is now available, due to the physical imperfections within the state of all creation, the perfect communion as it existed in Eden cannot be fully realized until either the death of the physical body or Jesus returns for His Church (1 Thess. 4:17). This is the "new covenant" between God and man, activated and sealed by the blood of the *Truly Perfect Substitutionary Blood Sacrifice* (Jesus). In this New Covenant, the Holy Spirit acts as a Guide unto spiritual truth (John 16:13).

Discussion Questions

1. Can you recall a time when God showed you **general grace**, preserving your life so you could one day accept Christ's gift of salvation?

Why Did Jesus Have to Die?

2. Can you recognize **prevenient grace**—the series of events leading up to your coming to Christ—in your life?

3. Describe that **effectual calling**, that blessed moment when your eyes were opened to the truth of the Gospel, and when you gave Jesus the reins of your life.

Chapter Eight

The Security of the Believer's Salvation

The doctrines surrounding the extent of the believer's eternal security in their salvation have caused a great deal of pain within the body of Christ and each believer. The struggle lies in the fact that we are constantly at the center of a battle between two natures. As new creatures, we must put to death the old carnal nature. However, though our new nature has no desire to sin, we are still susceptible to the temptations of this fallen world. As the saying goes, we may not be sinless, but we should sin less. While God has given us the power to overcome sin, we still fall short of the mark.

It is from this "falling short" that the arguments about our eternal security spring. How can a God who demands perfection possibly accept such imperfections in His children? How can God honor the New Covenant with people who break the agreement daily? While I can ask God's forgiveness for my sins, how long can He keep forgiving me for new sins every day before finally having enough of my disobedience and canceling the agreement? Answers to these questions do not lie in the "how." The answers are based upon the "Who."

Who Initiated the New Covenant?

Based upon our earlier study of the doctrine of election, it is plain to see that God, in His infinite love, chose YOU before

Why Did Jesus Have to Die?

He even laid the foundations of creation; the same God who saw the end from the beginning as a singularity, who had YOU in mind when He laid out His plan. This same God knew full well the sins that YOU have committed, are committing, and will commit. Nothing has caught Him by surprise. Moreover, because there was nothing YOU could do to save yourself, it was God who initiated the New Covenant and supplied the *Truly Perfect Substitutionary Blood Sacrifice*, His own Son, to die in place of YOU and forgave all YOUR sins: past, present, and future.

Though we could spend a great deal of time going through all the different views on this subject, it would only serve to distort the Scriptural facts as they pertain to the question of eternal security. While, yes, some verses in the Bible seem to say that a believer can lose his or her salvation, those verses must be taken entirely out of context to do so. The issue really comes down to the fact that everything in this fallen world runs on a merit-based system. However, we need to understand that, in God's economy, our merits have nothing to do with the security of our salvation. While our sins will affect our communion and feelings of closeness with God, the *fact* of our adoption into God's family remains unchanged and unchangeable.

Once again, Paul Enns has done a masterful job of stating what we need to understand in his textbook, *The Moody Handbook of Theology*:

Securing Work of the Father

"Believers are secure because the Father has chosen them to salvation from eternity past (Eph. 1:4). The Father predestined believers to come to the status of sonship in Christ (Eph. 1:5). The Father has the power to keep believers secure in their salvation (Rom. 8:28-30). The ones the Father foreknew, predestined, called, and justified are the same ones He brings to glorification in the future. None are lost in the process. The Father's love for believers also guarantees their security (Rom. 5:7-10).

Securing Work of the Son

"The Son has redeemed the believer (Eph. 1:7), removed the wrath of God from the believer (Rom. 3:25), justified the believer (Rom. 5:1), provided forgiveness (Col. 2:13), and sanctified the believer (1 Cor. 1:2). Moreover, Christ prays for believers to be with Him (John 17:24); He continues to be their Advocate at God's bar of justice (1 John 2:1); and He continues to make intercession as the believer's High Priest (Heb. 7:25). If a believer could be lost it would imply Christ is ineffective in His work as the believer's Mediator.

Securing Work of the Holy Spirit

"The Holy Spirit has regenerated the believer, giving him life (Tit. 3:5); the Holy Spirit indwells the believer forever (John 14:17); He has sealed the believer for the day of redemption (Eph. 4:30), the sealing being a down payment, guaranteeing our future inheritance; the believer is baptized into union with Christ and into the body of believers (1 Cor. 12:13).

"For a believer to lose his salvation would demand a reversal and an undoing of all the preceding works of the Father, Son, and Spirit. The key issue in the discussion of the believer's security concerns the issue of who does the saving. **If man is responsible for securing his salvation, then he can be lost; if God secures the person's salvation, then the person is forever secure.**

"The eternal security of the believer by the grace of God is the completion and crowning glory of God's plan of salvation." (pp. 340-41; emphasis added)

Given what Paul Enns so eloquently explained above, it should be clear to every believer that their eternal security is entirely and utterly assured by no less than the Triune God, Creator of the universe! So, why do so many doubt their salvation?

While teaching these doctrinal principles in my college classes and in a Sunday School setting, I never fail to be amazed at the number of Christians—people I know have been saved and bearing good fruit for the Kingdom—who, when asked, "Do you know that you will spend eternity in heaven?" give the depressing answer, "I hope so." The question then becomes, if our salvation is so secure, why are so many Christians feeling so insecure?

The answer is twofold:
1. We live in a merit-based world. If you want money, you must work and earn it. If you want to plant a garden that produces a good yield, you must work hard to keep it up. If you want a wife or husband to love you, you must reciprocate and show love in order to build a strong relationship. However, staying with this marriage analogy, would you feel secure in your marriage if you kept doing things that disappointed your spouse? In the same way, because we tend to ascribe the same merit-based model to spiritual matters, our inability to keep from sinning serves to make us feel insecure.

2. Satan knows that if you doubt your own salvation, you will not be inclined to share your faith with

The Security of the Believer's Salvation

others. Therefore, he uses that insecurity to great effect, whispering accusations into our ears. He hisses things like, "God could never love someone as wretched as you!" Or, "How could you possibly think you are worthy of forgiveness when you keep doing the same thing again and again?" Or, perhaps the hardest one to overcome, "So many people you know have walked away from their faith. You know they've gone too far and are lost again! What makes you think you're any better than them?"

Therefore, the question becomes, "How do I overcome my own feelings of inadequacy, as well as Satan's accusations, so I can feel secure in my salvation?" The answer here is twofold as well:

1. Keep reminding yourself of this fact: **There was nothing you could do to earn your salvation, so you can do nothing to keep it.** As I stated at the beginning of this study, this is in no way a license for unfettered sin! If you can go right on sinning without the conviction of the Holy Spirit, you were never saved in the first place! You may have made an emotionally-based decision **toward Christ** at some point, but that is far from placing your faith **in Christ**.

   The key is, when you sin, do you feel the conviction of the indwelling Holy Spirit about that sin? If not, you need to closely examine your spiritual condition. If you do feel that conviction, that is a proof of your salvation, albeit in a somewhat backhanded way.

2. To overcome Satan's accusations: First, do what you can to take away Satan's ammunition. Sin less!

Write down verses that remind you of who you are in Christ and speak them over yourself daily. The following are just a few I recommend: Phil. 2:5; Phil. 4:8; 1 Peter 1:13; Col. 3:2; and Romans 12:2.

Second, use your authority as a **child of the King**—a **prince** or **princess of the Kingdom of God** and a **co-heir with Christ** (Rom. 8:17)—and command Satan to shut up and leave you alone in the name of Jesus! **You have been cleansed by the most potent substance that has ever been—the precious Blood of Jesus**! You remind Satan that he is a defeated foe!

Discussion Questions

1. Have you struggled with this question of security in your life, and has it affected your ability to share the Gospel with others?

2. After reading about your eternal security being assured by each Person of the Trinity, did that help you to understand the issue in a new way? If so, how?

3. Do you now feel better about your standing in the Kingdom of God? Does that make you appreciate what Jesus did for you to a greater extent, and does that make you want to follow Him closer?

Chapter Nine

What Salvation is Not

Faith-Plus Religious Systems

Now that we have firmly established the Scriptural truths surrounding the doctrine of salvation (soteriology), we must be prepared to recognize the numerous pseudo-Christian religious systems that have peppered the religious landscape and infiltrated nearly every Christian denomination that exists. Each of these religious systems has unique beliefs and practices, which are too many to cover fully here. However, they all share one primary trait: the faith-plus doctrine.

Faith-plus, in essence, means that to attain salvation, the believer must have faith; **plus**, they must perform at a specified level of piety, act a certain way, contribute at a certain level (either with their time, money, or both), or meet any other criteria to satisfy their particular brand of "Christianity" and, therefore, merit forgiveness. The best examples generally come from real-life illustrations. Therefore, I will relate a story involving a good friend of mine:

> My friend came to me one day with great joy in his heart. He had found Jesus and was basking in the new life he had received. I was so happy for him and encouraged him in his new faith. Also, knowing that Satan loves to squelch the joy of new believers, I told

him that I was always available if he had any questions, concerns, or struggles.

Only two days later, I received a call from my friend, who was suddenly depressed to the point of tears. He told me his pastor at a famously hard-lined Pentecostal church told him his salvation was incomplete until he "spoke in tongues." He said that he had spent the last two days trying as hard as he could to receive this gift of the Spirit but to no avail. He was desperate and devastated.

I tried my best to talk him down from the spiritual ledge to which his pastor led him, but because I did not hold a pastoral office of any kind, he refused to take my word over that of his pastor. I gave him verse after verse of Scripture to appease his worries over his eternal security. However, nothing helped because his pastor had already warned him that other "so-called Christians" would do exactly what I was doing.

How tragic that a pastor would lead a man to pure joy only to pull it away and leave him in worse spiritual turmoil than he had been in before. This so-called "pastor" is guilty of foisting a faith-plus religious system upon his parishioners. In his view, faith, plus the gift of "speaking in tongues," equals salvation, and this view is based solely on one verse that he had to twist to make it align with his equally twisted view. This heresy goes against everything that Jesus' work on the Cross achieved. Paul sternly warned the believers at Galatia about such deceivers:

> "I marvel that you are turning away so soon from Him who called you in the grace of Christ, to a different gospel, which is not another; but there are some who trouble you and want to pervert the Gospel of Christ. But even if we, or

What Salvation is Not

an angel from Heaven, preach any other gospel to you than what we have preached to you, let him be accursed. As we have said before, so now I say again, if anyone preaches any other gospel to you than what you have received, let him be accursed." Gal. 1:6-9

Please understand my point here. I am not laying all fault at the feet of this one pastor or denomination. All cult and pseudo-Christian religions stand under this same basic faith-plus doctrinal banner. A quick study of Jim Jones, David Koresh, Jehovah's Witnesses, Mormons, Islam, and, sadly, many "Christian" denominations and sects have this one fatal flaw, and in many of these cases, multiple fatal flaws, in common. If any requirement of works is added to faith to attain salvation, it is a false gospel.

Things That DO NOT Equal Salvation

- **Rote or Prescribed Prayers-** If anyone tells you that your sins will be forgiven by reciting a specific prayer, especially if they tell you to use some religiously imbued item in unison with that prayer, this in no way cleanses you of sin and leads to salvation. Faith in Christ, and faith alone, leads to salvation.

- **Confession of Sins to a Priest-** We are to confess our sins to God, asking His forgiveness with a repentant heart. Doing this in faith is always good for an existing believer who has already attained salvation. However, the Bible has never prescribed confessing sins to a man or priest. Also, doing so is never a proof of salvation.

- **Baby Baptism, Sprinkling, or Dedication-** It may be as cute as anything could be to dress a baby in their finest clothes and perform a ritual sprinkling

Why Did Jesus Have to Die?

or baptism over them, but it in no way equals that child's salvation. A baby's dedication has a more functional purpose, but one that has more to do with the obligations of the adults in that child's life than it does the child's eternal security. These dedications are right and good. However, that child must still make his or her choice to follow Christ in order to attain salvation.

- **Believer's Baptism-** To be clear, the baptism of a believer is a very important rite that EVERY new believer should do as immediately as possible after placing their faith in Christ! This is the model prescribed in several places in the book of Acts when the fledgling Church was begun after Pentecost. In Jesus' own words, in the Great Commission (Matt. 28:16-20; Mark 16:14-18; Luke 24:44-49; John 20:19-23; Acts 1:4-8), He commands the disciples to go to all nations, make disciples, and baptize them in the name of the Father, Son, and Holy Spirit. However, the very closeness of the relation to salvation and baptism has led to the idea that one cannot have one without the other. It must be stated emphatically: You can be saved without being baptized, and you can be baptized without being saved! The thief on the Cross next to Jesus was guaranteed salvation by Christ (Luke 23:43) but was not baptized. In fact, Paul, one of the greatest evangelists in history, is even thankful that he did not baptize many of those he led to Christ (1 Cor. 1:14) because they would follow him more than Jesus. But if salvation was not complete unless baptism was performed, why did he leave them unbaptized?

It must also be said that I personally know many who hold to the erroneous view that baptism and salvation are linked as one event, and I know them to be great men and women of faith. However, adding any ritual to faith as being necessary to attain salvation is not biblically sound. It can only seem so by taking several verses out of clear context, as well as ignoring several verses which never mention baptism as a requirement for salvation.

- **Speaking in Tongues** (erroneously called "the baptism of the Holy Spirit")- This gift of the Holy Spirit is probably the most misunderstood facet of the New Covenant ethos. The ideologies surrounding "tongues" have sparked more infighting and division within the Church than almost any other, and if we tried to plumb its depths, we would become hopelessly off course from our primary objective. Suffice it to say, ANY gift of the Holy Spirit would be a gift from the Spirit that is already in residence within an existing believer, not a requirement of salvation. It would actually be a work added to faith in that context.

- **Any Other Religious, Physical, Monetary, or Time Requirement-** If any church or religious organization prescribes any form of spiritual, physical, fiscal, or temporal act, rite, or checklist to be performed before eternal salvation can be attained, RUN! In fact, for reasons too many to discuss here, I can guarantee that those religious entities either diminish or deny the Trinity altogether!

One Other Very Concerning Cult Gaining Following:
"Progressive Christianity"

"Progressive Christianity" is an insidious trend being popularized at an alarming speed, digging its black claws into many mainstream churches and denominations. This twisted view of "Christianity" adheres only to those teachings of Christ which align with popular culture and the many new religions that arise from the hard left, socialistic, and Marxist elements of our society. Progressive Christianity is neither progressive nor Christianity! It is, in fact, quite regressive and satanic! Of late, it is being marketed politically as "inclusive democracy."

I separate this abomination from the faith-plus religious systems because, in this system, faith in Christ is completely replaced with faith in any and all religious systems other that biblical Christianity, spending their time as warriors on behalf of humanistic endeavors (self-worship), "women's reproductive rights" (abortion on demand, even after birth), "social justice" (Not-so-cleverly-disguised racism and fascism), "gender affirming care" (contributing and aiding the mentally ill—and children, who should be protected from just such predatory behavior—in order to facilitate gender mutilation), homosexual rights and the lowering of the age of consent (more mentally ill and child predatory behavior), black/brown liberation theology (more racist behavior), illegal immigration (law breaking), as well as anything else of which the Bible calls abhorrent and abominable.

If any of the items on this list have you thinking, "Well, that isn't as bad as all that," then I would suggest that the normalization of such anti-Christ pursuits has taken a greater hold than you may believe! I will not apologize for such a firm, blunt stance on these issues! If I truly love, I **MUST** warn people about the hot stove they are about to touch! Be informed, test the spirits, and know what and why you believe!

Discussion Questions

1. Have you recognized any faith-plus entities as such through reading the information above? What have you heard must be added to faith in order to attain salvation?

2. Have you been adding something to your own faith in order to feel as though you are saved?

3. Will you share what you've learned in this study to help others realize the freedom they have in Christ?

Chapter Ten

The Hope We Have in Christ!

> *"For the believer there is hope beyond the grave, because Jesus Christ has opened the door to heaven for us by His death and resurrection."*
>
> —Billy Graham

We have covered a great deal of ground thus far, to say the least! And, while the doctrines of salvation are of great and wonderful benefit to the living, the study would not be complete without fully exploring the benefits to those who have, and eventually will have, slipped beyond the veil. Therefore, in this final chapter, we will summarize what we now know about how we will get to Heaven. Then, we will discuss the resplendently magnificent rewards that await us!

Summary Statement

Given what we have discussed in this study, we can now see that:

- God created a perfect world in which man had perfect communion with Him.

Why Did Jesus Have to Die?

- The Fall brought about a break in that communion and a loss of eternal life (both physical and spiritual).

- God promised a coming Messiah (Savior) who would set everything right again.

- Faith in God's promised Messiah became the requirement for salvation (Old and New Testaments).

- Because blood is the sealing agent of any covenant between man and God, only a *Truly Perfect Substitutionary Blood Sacrifice* could fully reverse the damage of the Fall.

- Jesus was the promised Messiah, lived a perfect life, and satisfied all the requirements of a *Truly Perfect Substitutionary Blood Sacrifice* when He willingly died on the Cross, atoning for all sins (past, present, and future).

- Due to Jesus' work on the Cross, every person has been drawn to the point of decision through the calling of the Holy Spirit; has been given the opportunity to place his or her faith in Christ to become a member of God's elect (foreknown by God before creation); and, upon that decision to place their faith in Christ, have been indwelt and sealed by the Holy Spirit, and regenerated as a "new creature" in Christ.

- Because of the New Covenant, which was initiated by God the Father; carried out through Jesus' death, burial, and resurrection; and sealed with Jesus' blood by the Holy Spirit, the believer has achieved forgiveness of sins in this life and full exoneration in the next life.

- Every true believer can be assured of their eternal security because God Himself (the Trinity in perfect agreement) has done all the work to affect that security.

- And finally, believers must beware of "faith-plus" religious systems that have, and are, infiltrating the modern Church—thereby blaspheming the finished work of Jesus on the Cross.

What Wonders Await!

> *"And he showed me a pure river of water of life, clear as crystal, proceeding from the throne of God and of the Lamb. ² In the middle of its street, and on either side of the river, was the tree of life, which bore twelve fruits, each tree yielding its fruit every month. The leaves of the tree were for the healing of the nations. ³ And there shall be no more curse, but the throne of God and of the Lamb shall be in it, and His servants shall serve Him. ⁴ They shall see His face, and His name shall be on their foreheads. ⁵ There shall be no night there: They need no lamp nor light of the sun, for the Lord God gives them light. And they shall reign forever and ever."* Revelation 22:1-5

I must admit, the thought of what to expect in Heaven can be intimidating, overwhelming, or downright beyond my finite mind to form a picture that would do it justice. The truth is, I am in good company! I have gone as far as saying, "I'll find out when I get there. Otherwise, trying to imagine it is just silly since I'm probably wrong anyway." However, while that may be true in large part, there are some things we can find or infer from Scripture about our final reward. The tough thing about describing Heaven is rooted in the fact that we have nothing on which to base any comparisons. Nevertheless, I shall try my best.

1. **What Should We Expect During the Transition?**

I suppose it would be logical to start at the very end of this life, stepping into the next. Much has been written and told describing this wondrous transition. We have all heard about the "dark tunnel with the beautiful, loving light at the end." As a theologian, I can only be adamant about those things which are confirmed in Scripture which, in no place speaks about any "tunnel." It isn't that I disbelieve it. There just isn't any biblical corroboration.

I will say this: if true, it makes some sense. As we step from our sinful, sin-sick, and decaying bodies—these suitcases for our souls—that might explain the darkness of the "tunnel." And, that ultra-bright, warm, and loving light at the end—a light which overtakes the darkness behind—could very well be the Lord-given light described in the verses cited above. We cannot say for sure if this is so, but there also aren't any Scriptures that denounce this idea.

2. **What Should We Expect When We Get There?**

Popular culture has given us ideas of Heaven that are just plain silly! Movies, the arts, and pervasive new-age ideas have brought about visions of playing harps while floating on cotton-ball clouds. There are also the sweet little, fat cherubs depicted in paintings, which may look cute, but are better suited as gaudy garden statuary than anything approaching the throne room of God. Then we have the new-age pictures of an ethereal, heaven-like existence, a refolding of our essences back into the cosmic stream, perhaps even coming back as a snail or a tree. However,

The Hope We Have in Christ!

from Scripture, there are many things we can know about Heaven. These are just a few:

- We can expect a place designed and built just for us by the hands of the Carpenter Himself! (John 14:2; 2 Cor. 5:1)

- We can expect rewards for the things we did for God and others with unselfish motivations and intentions. (Col. 3:23-24; Matt 16:27; 1 Cor. 3:8; Matt. 6:19-21)

- We can expect our names written in the *Book of Life*. (Rev. 3:5) I know this is a given, but I personally can't wait to see that!

- We can expect to meet our brothers and sisters in Christ—our true and eternal family. This point needs to be expounded upon due to the depth of this subject.

"For now we see in a mirror, dimly, but then face to face. Now I know in part, but then I shall know just as I also am known." (1 Cor.13:12)

The above verse is Paul explaining that, when he gets to Heaven, he will then know Jesus just as Jesus now knows him. That in and of itself is going to be amazing! However, it also has implications which will apply to all of our brothers and sisters in Christ—even the ones we have never met in this life!

In fact, if we know them as well as Jesus knows us, it would mean that a brother in Christ who lived in Mongolia 400 years ago will be as close, or closer, than my actual brother here on earth! Now, multiply that by billions of Christians since the birth of the Church, and beyond. Isaiah will be closer to you than your own sister or brother! You and David will embrace as though you were a long-lost family member! Perhaps C. S. Lewis will tell me, "Since we're family, I feel I can tell you where you were wrong in your writing on the subject of election." I'm joking, of course. But the point is, You and I, though we have probably never met will forever be family! Personally, I cannot wait to meet you!

In conclusion

It is my firm hope that this study has been a blessing to you and has enabled you to see your salvation in a clear, glorious, and exciting new light. I often ask my students somewhere near the beginning of my teaching on Soteriology (the Doctrines of Salvation), "Who do you think you are in Christ?" I often get the pat answers, "I am loved," or "I am forgiven." Those answers are true, no doubt! However, at the end of those classes, after I've shown them all the things that you yourselves have just seen, the answers change dramatically! I have gotten something like this:

"I am a child of the King, Creator of the universe, who chose me before time began, and continues to choose me, love me, and empower me to live righteously through the power of the indwelling Holy Spirit! Jesus saved me, He is always with me, He has promised to keep me until the end, and He has prepared a wonderful place for me and all of you, the likes of which we can hardly imagine!"

I pray that you are all this excited about your gift of salvation! However, if you have yet to receive that gift from the hands of a loving Savior, I implore you to do it now! We are not guaranteed our next breath, and if you're not sure about the state of your eternal soul, now is the time to get that right.

It doesn't matter what kind of brokenness you bring to him. He is the Great Physician who can heal you, but only if you allow Him to do so. This is not a magic spell of any kind. But if you cry out in faith, God will make a change in you that will affect your entire outlook on life, yourself, and your eternity!

Go to Him in prayer now, confessing that you are a sinner in need of salvation, and ask Him to take the reins of your heart and make you a new creation.

If you have done this, welcome to the family!

The Professor's Prayer

I pray that God will use every person who participates in this study to fulfill the Great Commission and further the Kingdom of God on earth, thereby doing the good works that God has foreordained for each of His children to do.

I also pray that each of you, when confronted with worldly ideas of salvation by the unchurched and unscriptural notions of salvation within your local churches, will gently and humbly shepherd the confused into a better understanding of the greatest gift God has ever given to man!

In Jesus' name, amen.

Discussion Question

1. In what ways has your view of salvation changed in light of this study?

For Deeper Study

Though most of the ideas discussed in this study are derived from Scripture, further study of works by great men of faith is invaluable to students of any level of education in clearing up misunderstandings and seeing other perspectives. The following have been greatly informative and, in many cases, formative in my understanding of Scripture, the study of theology, and myself as a Christian:

> *Basic Theology: A Popular Systematic Guide to Understanding Biblical Truth* by Charles C. Ryrie; Moody Press, Chicago, Ill.; ©1999
>
> *The Moody Handbook of Theology* by Paul Enns; Moody Press; The Moody Bible Institute of Chicago; ©1989
>
> *Christian Theology* by Millard J. Erickson; Baker Academic, Grand Rapids, MI.; ©1998
>
> *Major Bible Themes* by Lewis Sperry Chafer, revised by John F. Walvoord; Zondervan Publishing House, Grand Rapids, MI.; ©1974

A good study Bible from a Scripturally solid writer and publisher. Try to steer clear of study Bibles from any groups who tend to be on the fringes of normative Christian theology (ultra-liberal, ultra-conservative, social or liberation theology, "name-it-and-claim-it," and "super-grace" based groups).

To order additional copies of

Why Did Jesus Have to Die?
A Biblical Study of Salvation
and the
Theological Implications of
Jesus
As
The Truly Perfect Substitutionary Blood Sacrifice

Go to www.godlyfiction7.com.

You can also browse other titles by T. B. Thornton

www.ingramcontent.com/pod-product-compliance
Lightning Source LLC
Chambersburg PA
CBHW061505040426
42450CB00008B/1496